One Summer Day

One Summer Day

Poems by

Eva Eliav

Cover design by Shay Culligan

ISBN: 978-1-954353-17-6

Kelsay Books
502 South 1040 East, A-119
American Fork, Utah, 84003

For Ehud

Acknowledgments

Many thanks to the publication in which versions of the following poems have appeared:

The Blue Nib Journal: Five Poems from "One Summer Day"

1

I'm shedding words

wake to find them
scattered across my pillow

follicles
silvery with dryness

2

last night you fell

the crash
and your moans
woke me

where
I ask
eyes shut

you understand

you answer
not my head

later we're fast asleep

our hands fitted together
like a joint

in the end we have the love
that we can manage

3

just before dawn

pigeons break
their nightlong fast
of silence

jolt us from sleep

voices pulsing
like a heavy metal band

eggs laid silently
in hidden nests

it's war I think
smuggling them away

pale and light
still warm

us or them

4

our terrace has become
a wilderness

pigeons nesting
on walls

in every cranny

they fly at me
from under crumbling pots
of half dead succulents

the summer dawn is bloated
with their cooing

5

muscular young men
will tame the terrace

scrape away
rusty leaves and
pigeon droppings

roots that have
claimed the terrace
as their own

possessive
clinging

young men will dismember them
without regret

6

I'm reading an article
about the luxury of a life
free of regret

only the word luxury
isn't mentioned

regret has become
my most faithful companion

I weep
too easily

bone and emotion
meld

I am a river

7

in my bag
a portable book of psalms

small as a child's fist

a gift from someone
who doesn't know you well

you tossed it over
like a hot potato

it's nesting in used tissues
a change purse
footlets
keys
lipgloss
insect repellent

spiky black letters
conjuring beauty

a woman's bag
equipped
to vanquish demons

8

sunlight wraps me
in its tourniquet

a neighbour waters plants
caresses flowers

an old man passes
with a garbage bin

the sidewalk cracks open
beneath his feet

he passes
unaware of devastation

I'm sitting at
a scarred wooden table

sipping
cool sweet morning

scribbling words

like starving beasts
devouring their own muscle

poems survive

9

strangers share my web
of rituals

we speak in covert glances
understandings

the same ants sting our feet

we bathe together
in the same hot wind

traffic rumbles by
the radio squawks

two boys are arguing
in Italian

a man and woman
fiddle with their phones

within this snarl
of languages and silence

we pulsing knots
of life

10

a busker's cradling
his violin

coaxing uncanny melodies

private yet shrill
as voices in the night

heat swaddles my limbs
I move slowly

years peel away
like flyers from a wall

11

street music

the whine of saws

the clamor
of birds disrupted

trees dismembered

with love
the laborers tell me

their biceps are thick
with muscle
slick with sweat

they wipe the grains
of wood dust
from their saws

12

a closed circuit
of moments

a fat white dog
is bouncing on its toes

the lights turn red
and green
and red again

children squabble
and a woman smokes

a jumble sale of details
unregarded

a poet needs the senses
of a bear

my eyes see shadows
and my ears confound me

13

I've been to the
flower shop

people who see me
carrying a begonia

will think all's calm
all's beautiful
in my world

14

rattling
inside my skull

small hard stones
of memory
disbelief

around me
stillness

the hot wind's slippery tongue

a red ant
climbs the crumbling tower
of my throat

15

I fill this space
barely
fearfully

an aging woman
in a flowered dress

words flicker like faulty neon
bright and dark

a lightening bug
within a flowered dress

16

a broad tree
shades my table

its canopy
frivolous with birds

its trunk thick
with muscles and tendons

a mighty arm

17

cruelties hide

like hermit crabs
in shelters they have stolen

in mouths that smile

in hands that soothe
and cook
and fondle children

too late you know
what shaped you

and misshaped you

the thought arrives
quietly as a spider

you are entangled

18

mosquitoes feed on me
invisible
efficient

soundlessly
smacking their lips

preserving their way of life
their generations

19

an ant attacks
my toe

we are natural enemies
the ant and I

I lash out
mindlessly

his blood's a thin red smear

20

I confess
all of it matters

the time of day
morning
afternoon

the place I settle

near but not too near
a flower box
where ants and mosquitoes lurk

the table clean
or stained

the angle of the sun
upon my feet

my sandals
a cat's cradle
or a slide

the flavour of the coffee
bitter
sweet

the story of my flesh
each cell's prognosis

21

a man is begging
a professional

patient
hovering

efficient as a mantis

a young girl wipes my table
shy and quick

pigeons cluster round
a wealth of crumbs

a cat spills to the pavement
like gray water

22

today isn't a good day
for words

I fantasize
giving enemas
to pens

23

a traffic jam
of words

nothing moves
nothing moves
nothing moves

the wind is mocking me
as it slides past

24

moments pass
weightless
as mosquitoes

a beetle's splashing
in a cup of water

I watch his struggles

thinking of fates
we can't be rescued from

a magpie scolds me
with its butter yellow beak

accuses me
with little hops
and flutters

of idleness
of despair

25

I don't believe scientists
who say
the sky is made of air

ethereal

it's as solid
as the sidewalk
beneath my feet

a stone god

body of pale marble
veined with gray

nails of yellow fire
clawing earth

26

there is a bookstore
on the corner

a man
rotund and pale
as a spirit bear

peers from his cave

lifts a paw
in greeting

I wander
into the dimness

sniff old paper

warm myself
at a bonfire of decay

27

I try to remember
how it felt
to believe in magic

an army in faded jeans
and untied sneakers

entering the fairy forest
before nightfall

28

a dove is visiting

more delicate than a pigeon
pink and gray

she picks her dainty way
between the tables

confident
transient as a shadow

29

the door opens
and the words engulf me

children expecting treats
of raw emotion

next time
I promise myself

I will refuse

30

I tap words
lightly

secretive green melons

listening for an echo
a vibration

I've heard wisdom
from the watermelon man

a hollow sound
means ripe

About the Author

Eva Eliav received a BA in English Language and Literature from The University of Toronto and completed her studies towards an MA in English and American Literature at the University of Tel Aviv. Her poetry and short fiction have been published in numerous literary journals both online and in print, including *Room, The St. Ann's Review, Emrys Journal, Ilanot Review, Flashquake, The Apple Valley Review, Stand Magazine, The Blue Nib, Horizon Review, Boston Literary Magazine, The Enchanted Conversation, Constellations,* and *Fictive Dream.* Her poetry collection, *Eve,* was published in spring 2019 by Red Bird Chapbooks.

www.ingramcontent.com/pod-product-compliance
Lightning Source LLC
Chambersburg PA
CBHW031155090426
42738CB00008B/1339